THE TASTE OF
FRANCE

WHSMITH

EXCLUSIVE
· BOOKS ·

Compiled by Frédéric Lebain and Jean-Paul Paireault
Photographed by Jean-Paul Paireault
Designed by Philip Clucas
Adapted and Translated by Lynn Jennings-Collombet

Acknowledgements

The publishers would like to thank the following for their valuable assistance and cooperation in the production of this book:

Madame Bayle, at Mas Le Plan in Lourmarin, for facilities for location photography.
The shopkeepers of Lourmarin and Pertuis for their special efforts to obtain and provide a variety of fresh and attractive fish, meats and general provisions.
Morcrette, and Villeroy and Boch for the loan of glassware and plates.
Cine Photo Provence, in Aix-en-Provence for film processing.
Kettie Artigaud for her help with general styling and furnishing.
Kathleen Jennings for her patience and help throughout the adaptation and translation of this book.
Monsieur Remande, director of l'Ecole Supérieure de Cuisine in Paris.
Chef Xavier Vallero and Chef Eric Trochon for permission to use a selection of their recipes.
Also to Monsieur and Madame Lebain, Monsieur David and Madame Marie-Solange Bezaunt, Madame Chardot, and Monsieur Bernard Bouton of Sougé.

CLB 2194
This edition published 1990 exclusively for W.H. Smith Ltd
Copyright © 1989 Colour Library Books Ltd, Godalming, Surrey, England
Typesetting by Words and Spaces, Rowlands Castle, Hants, England
Colour separation by Hong Kong Graphic Arts Ltd, Hong Kong

ISBN 0 86283 759 6

THE TASTE OF

FRANCE

Frederic Lebain · Jean Paul Paireault

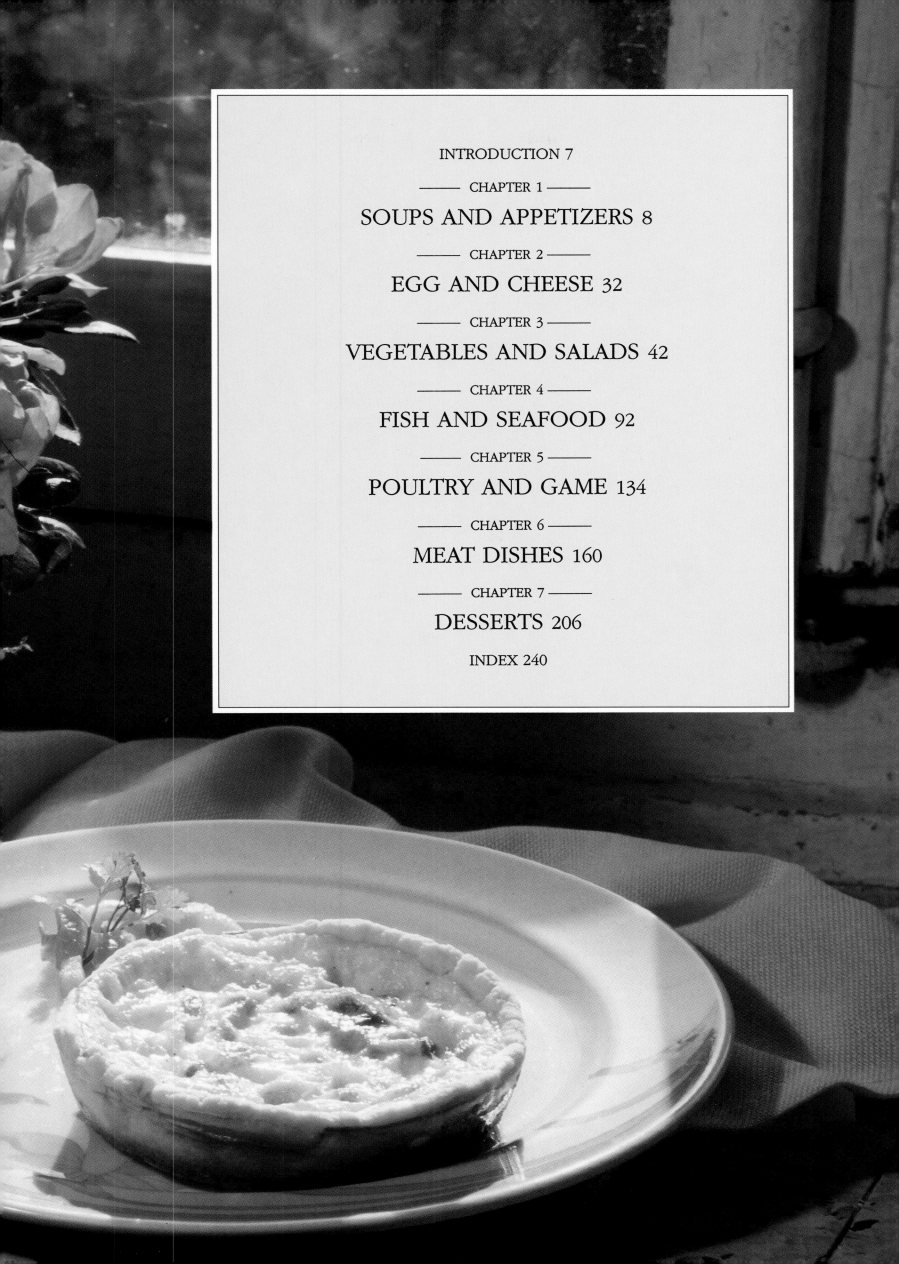

Introduction

The words 'food' and 'France' are almost synonymous. In no other country in the world does cooking have such a mystique as it does in France. Cooking is an art here, and not only in the *haute cuisine* restaurants of Paris. In fact, good food is such a part of ordinary, everyday life that the most famous and best-loved dishes are those that come from humble origins. For example, think of country pâtés, redolent of herbs, garlic and brandy; rich stews; hearty soups, and puddings made with pears, cherries or strawberries – the produce of local orchards and gardens.

Even though France has been reorganized into *départements*, the old provincial names – Normandy, Brittany, Champagne, the Loire, Ile-de-France, Alsace Lorraine, Burgundy, Bordeaux, Franche-Comté, Languedoc, Roussillon and Provence – still have special meaning where French cooking is concerned.

From Normandy, on the north coast, comes the richest milk, cream and butter. The province grows no wine, but its orchards produce cider apples from which Calvados, a fiery brandy, is made. Cider is a favourite drink, too, and dishes that combine it with apples and cream often bear the name 'Normande.'

Brittany's lambs graze on salt marshes, which gives their meat a distinctive flavour and forms the basis for a famous dish of roast or braised lamb with haricot beans. The region's best-known contribution, however, has to be crêpes. These thin pancakes are served with a variety of fillings, from cheese and ham to mixtures of local seafood.

The Champagne region has made a memorable gastronomic contribution – the world's most celebrated sparkling wine. The province is also known for its rich dishes with a Flemish influence and for a delicious savoury version of choux pastry called a *gougère*.

A lovely, fragrant wine comes from the Alsace region which, with its neighbour Lorraine, shares a fondness for hearty food that is very German in character. Foie gras and the rich pâté made from it are also produced here, and to drink there are varieties of eau de vie – kirsch, mirabelle and framboise, made from cherries, plums and raspberries, respectively.

The Loire flows through the heart of France. Walled kitchen gardens grow vegetables and herbs almost all the year round, while the vineyards produce delicate wines that complement the food of the region perfectly. The famous sauce, beurre blanc, a liaison of white wine, shallots and butter, originated here long before the *nouvelle cuisine* movement made it popular.

Ile-de-France, with Paris at its centre, is where *haute cuisine* was born. Because fine restaurants are what everyone thinks of first when visiting this region, its other assets are sometimes taken for granted. In the countryside surrounding Paris, hunting game is still very popular, and cooking it is an art. Mushrooms, both wild and cultivated, grow abundantly here, as do strawberries, while the rich pastures are home to the cows that help produce Brie.

Burgundy brings dishes such as Boeuf Bourguignon and Coq au Vin instantly to mind. We also have this province to thank for escargots, Dijon mustard and cassis, a blackcurrant liqueur, as well as for some of the finest wines anyone could hope to sample.

Franche-Comté is a mountainous region that abounds with game and ways of preparing it, while mountain streams provide delicious trout.

Bordeaux, like Burgundy, is known for its fine wines. It is also the place of origin for two well-known brandies – Cognac and Armagnac. Another famous product of the region is the truffle, which grows wild in the forests. Pâtés and terrines seem almost to have been invented with truffles in mind and the area boasts many delicious pâté recipes.

In the south lie Languedoc, Roussillon and, of course, Provence, the food of these provinces reflecting all the colour and warmth of the region. Languedoc has made cassoulets, casseroles of duck, pork or lamb with sausages and haricot beans, an important part of French cuisine. In Roussillon, the Spanish influence is stong and recipes use peppers and tomatoes freely. The flavour of Provence is one of herbs and garlic, sun-ripened tomatoes and good olive oil.

Each region in France has made its own important contribution to the national cuisine, so much so that it would be impossible to leave any one of them out. It is this wonderful combination of different tastes and styles of cooking that make us think of the pleasures of the table whenever we think of France.

--- SERVES 4 ---

CREAM OF TOMATO SOUP

*A rich and warming soup, ideal
for cold winter evenings.*

Step 2

Step 2

Step 2

□ 2kg/4½ lbs tomatoes, quartered   □ 1 onion, finely chopped
□ 2 ltrs/4 pints chicken stock   □ 1 clove garlic, halved
□ 1 sprig parsley, washed   □ 1 bay leaf   □ Pinch of thyme
□ 30ml/2 tbsps olive oil   □ Salt and pepper
□ Few drops Tabasco

1. Warm the olive oil in a frying pan and gently cook the tomatoes and onions until very soft.

2. Transfer to a large saucepan and add the parsley, garlic, thyme, bay leaf, salt and pepper. Then add the stock. Bring to the boil, stirring well, then reduce the heat and simmer gently for 1½ hours.

3. Allow the soup to cool, then remove the bay leaf and blend the soup in an electric blender until smooth.

4. Reheat before serving, adding a few drops of Tabasco.

TIME   Allow 5 minutes preparation time and at least 2 hours for cooking.

SERVING IDEAS   Decorate the soup by swirling through a little single cream.

VARIATION   Sprinkle over a few tablespoons of chopped fresh herbs, such as basil.

COOK'S TIP   The tomatoes can be seeded if preferred, although after blending the difference is negligible.

□

OPPOSITE

CREAM OF
TOMATO SOUP

LEEK AND POTATO SOUP

*An economical, tasty soup that
is quick and easy to prepare.*

□ 4 large leeks, thinly sliced   □ 4 large potatoes, peeled and
diced   □ 1 ltr/2 pints chicken stock
□ 450ml/1 pint water   □ Salt and pepper
□ 30g/2 tbsps butter   □ 60ml/4 tbsps double cream

TO SERVE

□ 60ml/4 tbsps single cream   □ 30ml/2 tbsps butter
□ 15ml/1 tbsp fresh chopped parsley
□ 15ml/1 tbsp fresh chopped chives

1. Melt 30g/2 tbsps butter in a frying pan and gently cook the leeks. Do not allow them to brown too much. Remove from the heat.

2. Transfer the leeks to a large saucepan, add the potatoes, stock, water, salt and pepper, bring to the boil, cover and reduce heat. Simmer for approximately 35 minutes.

3. Add the potatoes for the last 20 minutes of cooking.

4. Once cooked, stir in the double cream.

5. Either serve the soup as it is, or blend until smooth in a blender or food processor.

6. Serve in a large soup tureen, with the remaining butter dotted over and the single cream swirled over the top. Sprinkle over the herbs at the last minute.

TIME   Preparation of the vegetables takes about 10 minutes, cooking time is approximately 45 minutes and final touches take about 5 minutes.

VARIATION   Instead of leeks use a different vegetable, such as spinach or watercress.

SERVING IDEAS   To make the soup richer, add a few tablespoons of milk when stiring in the double cream.

□

OPPOSITE

LEEK AND
POTATO SOUP

AVOCADO PEARS
WITH CRAB

*Serve this delicately-flavoured starter
before a fish course; its success is assured.*

Step 2

Step 5

☐ 2 avocados   ☐ 1 small can crab meat
☐ 1 green pepper, seeded and pith removed
☐ 1 egg yolk, beaten   ☐ 175ml/6fl. oz oil (corn or similar)
☐ 5ml/1 tsp mustard   ☐ 30ml/2 tbsps tomato ketchup
☐ 1 drop Tabasco   ☐ 45ml/3 tbsps brandy
☐ Juice of 1 lemon   ☐ Salt and pepper

1. Begin by making the cocktail sauce. Beat together the egg yolk, mustard, salt, pepper, tomato ketchup, Tabasco and brandy. Then add the oil, drop by drop, beating continuously.

2. Peel the avocados and cut them in half. Remove the stone and coat the flesh with the lemon juice to prevent discoloration.

3. Cut the pepper into thin matchsticks.

4. Drain the crab meat.

5. Slice the avocados thinly and evenly and mix them with the pepper matchsticks. Arrange neatly on a serving plate.

6. Sprinkle over the crab meat and coat with the cocktail sauce.

TIME   Preparation takes approximately 25 minutes.

WATCHPOINT   Do not cut the avocados too far in advance as they may discolour even with the coating of lemon juice

VARIATION   Use fresh crab if time and budget permit.

☐

OPPOSITE

AVOCADO PEARS
WITH CRAB

——— SERVES 6 ———

ANCHOYADE

*This is an anchovy paste to spread on toast
and serve with a salad for a light meal.
Traditionally served in France for l'aperitif.*

☐ 15 salted anchovy fillets   ☐ 2 cloves garlic, peeled
☐ 100ml/4fl. oz olive oil   ☐ Few drops lemon juice

TO SERVE

☐ 1 prepared lettuce   ☐ 60ml/4 tbsps vinaigrette sauce
☐ 12 slices bread, toasted

Step 3

Step 5

1. Toss the lettuce in the vinaigrette sauce.

2. Rinse the anchovy fillets under cold running water to remove the excess salt. Pat them dry on kitchen paper.

3. Pound the garlic with a pestle and mortar until smooth.

4. Pound the fillets into the garlic until smooth.

5. Beat in the oil, a little at a time, until a smooth paste is formed.

6. Spread the mixture onto the slices of toast and place them on top of the tossed lettuce.

TIME   Preparation takes about 25 minutes.

VARIATION   The number of garlic cloves can be increased or decreased according to taste.

COOK'S TIP   Rinse the fillets very well. If they are extremely salty, soak for 1 hour in cold water before use.

PREPARATION   The anchoyade can be made in a blender – just put all the ingredients in together and blend until smooth.

☐

OPPOSITE

ANCHOYADE

—— SERVES 4 ——

HADDOCK MOUSSE

*A delicious, light mousse, delicately
flavoured by the smoked haddock.*

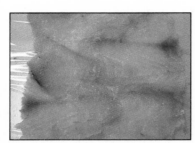
Step 7

Step 7

Step 8

☐ 3 smoked haddock fillets   ☐ 200ml/7fl. oz double cream
☐ 250ml/½ pint fish stock
☐ 15ml/1 tbsp fresh chives, chopped
☐ 3 leaves gelatin   ☐ Salt and pepper

1. Soak the gelatin in a bowl of cold water.

2. Cut one of the fillets in half and chop it finely. Use either a very sharp knife or a food processor.

3. In a saucepan, gently heat the fish stock and the chopped haddock fillet. Drain the gelatin sheets and stir into the stock until they have completely dissolved. Remove from the heat, transfer to a clean bowl and put in the refrigerator.

4. Meanwhile, whip the cream until it becomes light and fluffy. Keep cool.

5. Once the stock is completely cool, gently fold in the whipped cream, chives, salt and pepper.

6. Return mixture to the refrigerator for at least 2 hours.

7. Cut the remaining fillets into very thin slices and spread them out onto cling film. Place spoonfuls of mousse down the centre of each. There should be some mousse left over.

8. Using the cling film to help you, gently roll up the slices of haddock to make a neat roll.

9. Put the rolls back into the refrigerator until ready to serve.

10. Using a teaspoon, form the remaining mousse into small oblong shapes, and serve with the haddock roll. Remove the cling film before serving.

TIME   It will take approximately 1 hour to prepare the haddock mousse and 2 hours for it to set.

VARIATION   Use different herbs in the mousse to give alternative subtle flavours.

SERVING IDEAS   Serve a light dressing with the haddock, such as a blend of olive oil, lemon juice and a little salt and pepper.

☐
OPPOSITE

HADDOCK
MOUSSE

—— SERVES 6 ——

PEASANT'S SOUP

*A hearty vegetable soup, with a little bacon for
added flavour; great for meals on cold days.*

Step 4

☐ 1 ltr/2 pints chicken stock ☐ 150g/6oz leeks, chopped
☐ 200g/8oz potatoes, peeled and diced
☐ 100g/4oz cabbage, shredded
☐ 1 turnip, diced ☐ 100g/4oz smoked bacon, chopped
☐ 25g/1oz goose or other poultry drippings
☐ Salt and pepper

TO SERVE

☐ 4 slices of bread ☐ 100g/4oz Cheddar cheese, grated

1. Blanch the cabbage in boiling salted water. Drain well.

2. Shred the cabbage into a large saucepan and set aside.

3. In another saucepan, fry the bacon in the dripping and stir in all the vegetables except the potatoes.

4. Pour the stock over the shredded cabbage and bring to the boil. Transfer the bacon and vegetable mixture into the cabbage and stock. Season with salt and pepper.

5. Bring to the boil once again, cover, reduce the heat and simmer very gently for approximately 1½ hours.

6. Add the potato for the last 20 minutes of cooking. Check the level of the liquid during cooking; if it should get too low add a little water.

7. Sprinkle the cheese over the bread, and toast under a grill. Cut into small triangles or rounds and serve on a small plate with the soup.

TIME   Preparation takes about 15 minutes, and cooking takes about 1 hour and 50 minutes.

SERVING IDEA   Ladle the soup into individual bowls once it is cooked. Float the bread with the cheese sprinkled over on the top and brown under a grill.

WATCHPOINT   Check the liquid level carefully, adding water as necessary.

PREPARATION   Choose a good, fresh green cabbage for this simple but delicious soup.

☐

OPPOSITE

PEASANT'S SOUP

SERVES 6

CAULIFLOWER AND PARSLEY CREAM

Rich and creamy, this soup is a magical blend of cauliflower and parsley.

Step 4

Step 4

- □ 450g/1 lb cauliflower, washed and chopped
- □ 200g/8oz leeks, white part only, cut into thin slices
- □ 1 ltr/2 pints chicken stock
- □ 75ml/5 tbsps flat-leaved parsley, washed
- □ 200ml/6fl. oz double cream □ 50g/2oz butter

1. Melt half of the butter in a frying pan and cook the leeks until tender. Add the stock and the cauliflower.

2. Stir well and bring to the boil. Reduce the heat and simmer gently for 35 minutes. Retain 150ml/¼ pint of the soup for Step 4.

3. Blend the remainder of the soup with a hand mixer until smooth. Stir in the cream and the remaining butter, season well and set aside.

4. Blanch the parsley in salted boiling water, drain well and then, adding 2 tbsps of the cauliflower soup, blend with a hand mixer until smooth.

5. Serve the rest of the cauliflower soup in individual bowls, swirling the blended parsley over.

TIME   Preparation takes about 15 minutes and cooking takes approximately 50 minutes.

COOK'S TIP   The soup can be made in advance, kept in the refrigerator and reheated just before serving.

WATCHPOINT   The soup should be removed from the heat as soon as the cauliflower is cooked through in Step 2. Do not overcook; the 35 minutes mentioned is just an indication.

□

OPPOSITE

CAULIFLOWER AND
PARSLEY CREAM

PUMPKIN SOUP

*An unusual blend of sweet and sour flavours
go together to make a lovely soup.*

Step 1

Step 3

☐ 1.5kg/3 lbs pumpkin, peeled and cut into cubes
☐ 250ml/½ pint milk   ☐ 250ml/½ pint double cream
☐ 5ml/1 tsp cinnamon   ☐ Salt and pepper

1. Cook the pumpkin in boiling salted water until tender; approximately 20 minutes. Drain well.

2. Mash the pumpkin with a fork, stir in the milk, return to the heat and bring to the boil.

3. Blend with a hand mixer or in a liquidiser until smooth.

4. Reheat, remove from the heat, stir in the cream and cinnamon, and season well. Serve hot.

TIME   Preparation takes about 10 minutes, and cooking takes approximately 40 minutes.

WATCHPOINT   Make sure that you drain the pumpkin well, otherwise the soup will be too thin.

SERVING IDEAS   Decorate the soup by swirling over a few spoonfuls of single cream and sprinkling with chopped chives.

VARIATION   100g/4oz of grated Cheddar cheese added before reheating at Step 4 gives a pleasant flavour.

☐

OPPOSITE

PUMPKIN SOUP

---- SERVES 6 ----

ONION SOUP

*Traditionally consumed in the early hours after a night
out on the town, this is a hearty, nourishing soup.*

Step 1

☐ 100g/4oz butter ☐ 6 large onions, sliced ☐ Salt and pepper
☐ 1 ltr/2 pints chicken stock ☐ 4 slices bread, toasted
☐ 2 cloves garlic, crushed ☐ 100g/4oz grated cheese
☐ 100ml/6 tbsps white wine

1. In a large saucepan, melt the butter and cook the onion and garlic gently for approximately 30 minutes, stirring from time to time to prevent sticking. Add salt and pepper.

2. Remove from heat, stir in the wine and stock, return to the heat and bring to the boil, stirring continuously. Reduce heat and simmer for 30 minutes. If the soup appears too thick, stir in a little water.

3. Serve the soup in individual bowls. Cut the toast into cubes. Place the cubes on the soup, sprinkle over the grated cheese and place under a hot grill for a few minutes to melt the cheese.

TIME   Preparation takes 15 minutes and cooking takes 1 hour. To brown the top, an additional 5 minutes will be needed.

PREPARATION   Rub a clove of garlic over the toast before you cut it into cubes.

COOK'S TIP   If you do not have a grill, put the bowls into a very hot oven for a few minutes.

VARIATION   Red wine can be used instead of white, if desired.

☐

OPPOSITE

ONION SOUP

SERVES 4

HERBY GOAT CHEESE

Fresh goat's cheese is very popular in France, and is becoming more popular in other parts of the world. Its sometimes bland flavour is enlivened by the addition of herbs in this recipe.

□ 2 fresh goat cheeses   □ Few drops lemon juice
□ Few drops vinegar   □ 2.5ml/½ tsp olive oil   □ 10 capers
□ 5 peppercorns
□ 15ml/1 tbsp mixed fresh herbs, such as chives,
parsley and chervil
□ 15ml/1 tbsp finely chopped onion and shallot
□ Salt and pepper

Step 2

Step 3

1. Mix the cheeses with the chopped herbs, onion and shallot.

2. Mix in the capers, peppercorns and the salt and pepper.

3. Stir in the vinegar, lemon juice and olive oil. Stir well.

4. Place the cheese into 4 small ramekins, pushing it down well, and then set in the refrigerator for approximately 2 hours.

5. Turn out just before serving.

TIME   Preparation takes about 40 minutes.

SERVING IDEAS   Serve with a mixed salad tossed in vinaigrette sauce.

COOK'S TIP   Use only fresh goat cheese; avoid the dry variety which is often available, as it will crumble and will not mix in well.

□

OPPOSITE

HERBY GOAT
CHEESE

—— SERVES 4 ——

OMELETTES GOURMANDES

Lovely, rich-tasting omelettes, these are
perfect for a quick evening meal.

Step 3

Step 4

☐ 12 eggs, beaten   ☐ 4 onions, finely chopped
☐ 15ml/1 tbsp fresh herbs, chopped
☐ 100g/4oz mushrooms, sliced   ☐ 75ml/5 tbsps oil
☐ Salt and pepper

1. Sauté the onions in 30ml/2 tablespoons of oil over a high heat, then reduce the heat and cook for a further 20 minutes.

2. In another frying pan, sauté the mushrooms in 15ml/1 tablespoon of oil. Remove from the heat.

3. Add the beaten eggs to the mushrooms, stir in half of the onions, and cook over a high heat in as much of the remaining oil as necessary. Sprinkle over the herbs and cook the omelette until the base is crisp but the filling is still slightly liquid.

4. Fold one side of the omelette into the middle, then fold over the other side.

5. Serve on a bed of the remaining onions with a little salt and pepper.

TIME   It takes about 8 minutes to prepare the omelette and 8-10 minutes to cook it. Cooking time for the onions is about 20 minutes.

WATCHPOINT   Take care not to overcook the omelette; it should be served a little liquid in the centre.

SERVING IDEAS   Sprinkle a little diced red pepper around the edges of the omelette.

VARIATION   A multitude of ingredients can be added to omelettes; try chopped chicken livers, for example.

☐

OPPOSITE

OMELETTES
GOURMANDES

SERVES 4

SCRAMBLED EGGS
WITH OLIVES

*The addition of black olives to scrambled eggs
turns this simple dish into a memorable one.*

Step 1

Step 4

Step 5

☐ 12 eggs   ☐ 4 tomatoes, seeded and chopped
☐ 15 black olives, stoned   ☐ 1 clove garlic, chopped
☐ 100ml/4fl. oz olive oil   ☐ 1 small onion, chopped
☐ 25g/2 tbsps butter   ☐ Salt and pepper

1. Beat the eggs and set them aside.

2. Mince the tomatoes and the olives together finely using a food processor or mixer.

3. Warm the olive oil in a frying pan, increase the heat to high and cook the onion, garlic, tomatoes and olives until all the juices have evaporated.

4. Cook the eggs in the butter over a gentle heat, stirring continuously with a wooden spoon.

5. Once the eggs are cooked, stir in the tomato/olive mixture.

6. Serve on small, pre-warmed plates.

TIME   Preparation takes about 30 minutes and cooking takes 30 minutes.

SERVING IDEAS   Delicious with hot toast or muffins. Serve with salad and a fresh French stick for a light meal.

©Copyright F. LEBAIN

☐

OPPOSITE

SCRAMBLED EGGS
WITH OLIVES

—— SERVES 6 ——

CHEESE SOUFFLE

*This puffy, golden souffle will delight your
guests, but rush it to the table immediately
on removal from the oven!*

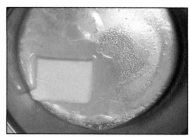

Step 2

Step 2

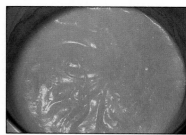

Step 3

☐ 25g/2 tbsps butter   ☐ 150g/6oz grated cheese
☐ 30g/1 tbsp plain flour   ☐ 250ml/½ pint milk
☐ Pinch of nutmeg   ☐ 4 eggs, separated
☐ 1 extra egg white   ☐ Butter for greasing   ☐ Salt and pepper

1. Preheat the oven to 200°C/375°F/Gas Mark 5. Grease a souffle dish with butter and sprinkle inside 3 tbsps of the grated cheese.

2. Melt the butter in a heavy saucepan, whisk in the flour, cook for about a minute, pour in all the milk and whisk continuously until the mixture thickens. Reduce the heat and cook for 2 minutes.

3. Add the salt, pepper, nutmeg and the egg yolks one by one, beating well with a wooden spoon. Leave to cool for about 5 minutes.

4. Stir the remaining cheese into the white sauce. Whisk the 5 egg whites until firm. Fold them gently into the cheese mixture with a metal spoon.

5. Pour the mixture into the prepared souffle dish and cook in the oven for 40-45 minutes.

6. The souffle should be well risen and golden-topped. Serve immediately.

TIME   Preparation takes approximately 20 minutes, and cooking takes 40-45 minutes.

SERVING IDEAS   At Step 5 the mixture could be poured into 6 individual buttered and "cheesed" ramekins. Cooking time will be reduced to 20-25 minutes.

VARIATION   50g/2oz cup crumbled blue cheese gives an unusual, but pleasant, flavour.

☐

OPPOSITE

CHEESE SOUFFLE

——— SERVES 6 ———

SAUERKRAUT SALAD

*A salad from the Alsace region, where the German
influence in the cooking is unmistakable.*

Step 2

Step 2

☐ 700g/1½ lbs cooked, fresh sauerkraut, pre-soaked for 2 hours
in cold water ☐ 2 carrots, grated ☐ 75ml/5 tbsps olive oil
☐ 30ml/2 tbsps wine vinegar ☐ 1 red apple, diced
☐ 2 small onions, chopped ☐ 5ml/1 tsp sugar
☐ 5ml/1 tsp cinnamon ☐ 2.5ml/½ tsp salt
☐ Pepper ☐ Juice of 1 lemon

1. In a large salad bowl, mix together the oil, vinegar, sugar,
pepper, cinnamon and salt until all the sugar and salt has
dissolved.

2. Wash the sauerkraut in cold water and drain well. Remove any
excess moisture with a dry tea towel. Cut the dry sauerkraut into
even lengths.

3. Pour the lemon juice over the apple, onion and carrot.

4. Mix all the ingredients together in the salad bowl, turning well
to incorporate the sauce.

TIME Pre-soak the sauerkraut for at least 2 hours. It takes
about 20 minutes to prepare this salad.

SERVING IDEAS In Alsace this salad is often served with slices
of sweetbread sausage.

VARIATION Add a little German sausage or liver sausage, cut
into small cubes.

WATCHPOINT Make sure the apple is well coated with the
lemon juice to prevent discoloration.

PREPARATION This salad can be made in advance and kept in
the fridge, but add the diced apple just before serving.

☐

OPPOSITE

SAUERKRAUT
SALAD

SERVES 6

FISHERMAN'S SALAD

A new dish to serve as an elegant starter to any meal. Care must be taken in the preparation of the vegetables, but the stunning result makes it well worth the effort.

Step 1

Step 1

Step 1

☐ 1 carrot, scraped   ☐ ½ cucumber, wiped, peeled and seeded
☐ 1 red pepper, seeded   ☐ 1 courgette, wiped
☐ About 40 small prawns, peeled (retain peelings)
☐ 15ml/1 tbsp olive oil   ☐ 15ml/1 tbsp brandy or cognac
☐ 175ml/6fl. oz single cream   ☐ Juice of ½ lemon
☐ 30ml/2 tbsps fresh chervil, chopped

1. Cut each of the vegetables carefully into thin strips. As you finish each vegetable, put the strips in the fridge to keep them crisp and fresh.

2. Fry the prawn peelings briskly over a high heat for 5 minutes in the olive oil. Add the brandy or cognac and flambé the mixture. Allow the alcohol to burn out, then stir in the cream, and continue cooking over a low heat for about 10 minutes.

3. Strain the sauce through a fine sieve, discarding all but the smooth sauce. Blend the sauce with a hand mixer and then put the sauce in the fridge to cool.

4. On a serving dish, spread a single bed of the vegetable strips and sprinkle over the peeled prawn.

5. Add the lemon juice to the cooled sauce, stir well and pour it over the salad. Sprinkle over the chervil and serve.

TIME   Preparation takes about 35 minutes.

COOK'S TIP   The sauce can be made in advance and kept in the fridge.

PREPARATION   Vegetables can be prepared on the morning of serving the dish, and kept covered in the fridge.

© Copyright F. Lebain

☐

OPPOSITE

FISHERMAN'S
SALAD

BUTTERED CABBAGE

*A great way of serving the humble cabbage. The
addition of bacon and onion adds a delicious flavour.*

Step 1

Step 1

☐ 1.5kg/3 ¼ lbs cabbage, shredded
☐ 225g/8oz smoked bacon, chopped
☐ 1 medium onion, chopped
☐ 100g/4oz goose or other poultry dripping or lard
☐ 100g/4oz butter ☐ Salt and pepper

1. Blanch the cabbage in boiling salted water. Drain well.

2. Melt the dripping or lard in a large frying pan. Add the bacon,
onion and cabbage, and stir well.

3. Cover and cook over a very gentle heat for 20 minutes.

4. Stir in the butter and cook for a further 20 minutes, covered.

5. Serve on a pre-heated serving dish.

TIME   Preparation takes about 10 minutes and cooking takes
about 45 minutes

WATCHPOINT   Ensure that the cabbage is well drained after
blanching.

COOK'S TIP   Do not use the outer leaves of the cabbage as
they are usually hard and bitter.

☐

OPPOSITE

BUTTERED
CABBAGE

—— SERVES 6 ——

FRICASSEE DE CAROTTES

*Sautéed carrots, gently cooked
with onions and smoked bacon.*

- 1.5kg/3 ⅓ lbs carrots, peeled and finely sliced into rounds
- 450g/1 lb onions, finely sliced   - 1 bouquet garni
- 45ml/3 tbsps goose or poultry dripping
- 300g/12oz smoked bacon, diced   - 5ml/1 tsp sugar
- 2.5ml/½ tsp cinnamon   - Salt and pepper

Step 1

1. In a large, heavy-based frying pan, gently melt the goose or poultry dripping, then increase the heat and sauté the carrots, onions and bouquet garni.

2. Shake the pan from time to time to prevent sticking. Once the vegetables begin to colour, reduce the heat, cover and cook for 25-30 minutes.

3. Blanch the bacon in boiling water, drain well and add to the carrot mixture.

4. Sprinkle over the sugar and cinnamon, cover and continue to cook until very tender.

Step 3

TIME   Preparation takes about 25 minutes and cooking takes approximately 1 hour.

SERVING IDEAS   Sprinkle over a little chopped chive or parsley.

WATCHPOINT   Cook the carrots very gently so that they do not dry out.

OPPOSITE

FRICASSEE DE
CAROTTES

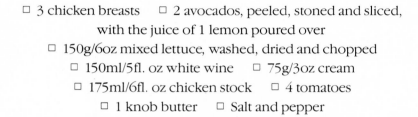

—————— SERVES 6 ——————

CHICKEN BREAST SALAD

*An eye-catching presentation of tomato, avocado,
lettuce and golden chicken breast, this salad
is a filling starter for a light main course.*

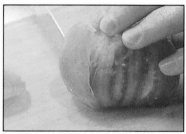

Step 4

Step 4

Step 4

☐ 3 chicken breasts   ☐ 2 avocados, peeled, stoned and sliced,
with the juice of 1 lemon poured over
☐ 150g/6oz mixed lettuce, washed, dried and chopped
☐ 150ml/5fl. oz white wine   ☐ 75g/3oz cream
☐ 175ml/6fl. oz chicken stock   ☐ 4 tomatoes
☐ 1 knob butter   ☐ Salt and pepper

1. Melt the butter in a frying pan and quickly seal the chicken on
all sides. Deglaze the frying pan with the white wine, pour over
the stock and cook over a moderate heat until the stock reduces
by half.

2. Reduce the heat to as low as possible, cover the pan and cook
for a further 8 minutes. Remove from the heat.

3. Set the chicken breasts aside, return the pan to the heat, stir in
the cream, and season with salt and pepper. Stir continuously
until the sauce thickens somewhat.

4. Peel two of the tomatoes, seed them, cut them into thin sticks
and then dice them.

5. Cut the remaining 2 tomatoes into thin slices.

6. Interlace the tomato slices and the avocado slices around a bed
of lettuce. Place the sliced chicken breasts in the middle. Dot the
diced tomato over and pour over the sauce.

TIME   Preparation takes about 30 minutes and cooking takes
approximately 30 minutes.

VARIATION   Toss the lettuce in a little vinaigrette sauce before
use.

WATCHPOINT   Coat the slices of avocado really well with the
lemon juice to prevent too much discoloration.

☐

OPPOSITE

CHICKEN
BREAST SALAD

— SERVES 6 —

SMOKED HERRING SALAD

*A nouvelle cuisine recipe especially developed
for the sophisticated dinner party.*

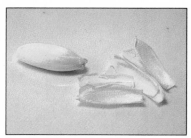

Step 1

Step 1

☐ 4 smoked herring, filleted   ☐ 4 large new potatoes, cooked
☐ 1 onion, finely chopped   ☐ 3 chicory/Belgian endives, wiped
☐ 8 coriander seeds   ☐ 150ml/5fl.oz olive or corn oil
☐ 5ml/1 tsp mustard   ☐ 15ml/1 tbsp wine vinegar
☐ 5ml/1 tsp sea salt   ☐ Pepper

1. Separate the chicory leaves and slice them lengthwise into thin strips.

2. Slice the herring fillets lengthwise and mix with the chicory leaves.

3. Dice the potatoes, mix with the above and add the onion, coriander seeds and salt.

4. In a salad bowl, mix together the oil, mustard, vinegar and pepper.

5. Add all the other ingredients and mix well to incorporate the sauce.

TIME   Preparation takes approximately 35 minutes.

COOK'S TIP   Always store chicory in semi-darkness, otherwise the leaves tend to turn green.

WATCHPOINT   Do not leave chicory to soak when cleaning them, as they have a tendency to become bitter.

VARIATION   Use smoked salmon instead of smoked herring.

☐

OPPOSITE

SMOKED
HERRING SALAD

FENNEL RAMEKINS

*These light fennel moulds are easy to prepare and cook
and, with their aniseed flavour, provide an original dish.*

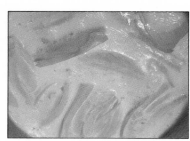

Step 1

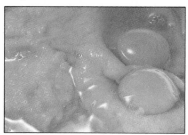

Step 3

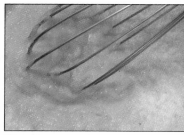

Step 3

☐ 900g/2 lbs fennel bulb, cut into quarters ☐ 4 eggs, beaten
☐ 1 ltr/2 pints milk
☐ 15ml/1 tbsp Pernod, or other aniseed alcohol
☐ 200ml/6 fl. oz double cream ☐ Salt and pepper
☐ A little butter for greasing

1. Cut off any hard patches from the fennel and discard them. Cook the fennel in the milk for about 30 minutes, then leave to drain well.

2. Once the fennel is well drained, put the quarters into a blender and blend until smooth – this should give about 500ml/1 pint of pulp. If necessary, make up to the desired amount by adding some of the cooking milk.

3. Whisk in the eggs, aniseed, cream, salt and pepper.

4. Butter 6 ramekin dishes and fill ¾ full with the fennel mixture.

5. Place the ramekins in a high-sided dish, add water to come halfway up the sides of the ramekins, and cook in a warm oven for 30-40 minutes.

6. To serve, turn the flans out of the ramekins onto a preheated serving plate.

TIME   Preparation takes about 10 minutes, and cooking takes approximately 1 hour.

WATCHPOINT   Make sure the fennel is well cooked and that you have exactly 500ml/1 pint of the purée.

SERVING IDEAS   Serve the moulds to accompany roast beef.

☐

OPPOSITE

FENNEL RAMEKINS

SPRING SALAD

The very pretty "rose" in the centre of this light salad
makes it a winning starter for a dinner party.

Step 1

Step 2

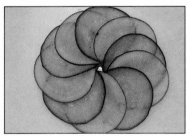

Step 2

☐ 1 head of lettuce, washed and shredded
☐ 1 cucumber, wiped and evenly sliced
☐ 1 horseradish root, washed and evenly sliced
☐ 3 tomatoes, seeded and evenly sliced
☐ 300g/12oz can tuna fish, drained ☐ 6 spring onions
☐ 12 black olives, stoned ☐ A few sprigs of fresh mint
☐ 200ml/7fl. oz olive oil ☐ 90ml/6 tbsps wine vinegar
☐ 3 drops Tabasco ☐ Salt and pepper

1. Prepare all the vegetables, taking special care with the cucumber and horseradish as this will be the centrepiece of your finished salad.

2. On a large, round serving plate, arrange the tuna fish in a round and then form a rose shape on top of the fish by interlacing cucumber and horseradish slices.

3. In a blender or food processor, blend the olives, spring onions, mint leaves, olive oil, Tabasco, vinegar, salt and pepper until smooth.

4. Place the shredded lettuce around the rose, followed by the tomatoes, and then pour over the olive/mint mixture.

TIME   Preparation takes about 45 minutes.

COOK'S TIP   Add a little more olive oil if the sauce is too thick.

SERVING IDEAS   The idea of the 'rose' presentation is optional, but the final effect is well worth the effort.

☐

OPPOSITE

SPRING SALAD

SERVES 8

SURPRISE POTATOES

These potatoes are an excellent and filling accompaniment to fish dishes.

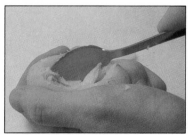

Step 2

Step 4

☐ 2kg/4½ lbs new potatoes, steamed (but not peeled)
☐ 100g/4oz butter ☐ 200ml/6fl. oz double cream
☐ 1 red pepper, seeded and cut into thin strips
☐ 15ml/1 tbsp olive oil ☐ Salt and pepper

1. Cook the pepper strips in the olive oil over a high heat for a few minutes. Remove from heat and set aside.

2. Cut the potatoes in half and remove the pulp, retaining the skins.

3. Work the butter, cream, salt and pepper into the potato pulp. Stir in the pepper strips.

4. Spoon the mixture back into the skins and warm in a hot oven for 5-8 minutes. Serve piping hot.

TIME   Preparation takes about 15 minutes and cooking takes about 30 minutes, including the cooking of the potatoes.

COOK'S TIP   The potatoes can be cooked in advance and stored in the refrigerator.

VARIATION   A little grated cheese can be srpinkled over the potatoes before the final 5-8 minutes in the oven.

☐

OPPOSITE

SURPRISE
POTATOES

PETITS POIS A LA FRANÇAISE

*Fresh peas cooked with onions and carrots
make a colourful vegetable combination to
accompany a wide variety of dishes.*

☐ 1kg/2 ¼ lbs fresh peas (about 3kg/7 lbs in the pod)
☐ 6 onions, finely chopped   ☐ 1 lettuce, finely shredded
☐ 2 carrots, peeled and finely diced   ☐ 10ml/2 tsps sugar
☐ 50g/2oz butter   ☐ 1 bouquet garni   ☐ Salt and pepper

1. Rinse the peas under cold water and leave to drain.

2. In a heavy-based saucepan, melt the butter and gently cook the peas, lettuce, onion, sugar, bouquet garni, salt and pepper for 5 minutes.

3. Increase the heat, add 2.5cm/1 inch water, bring to the boil and add the carrots.

4. Cover the saucepan, reduce the heat to very low and cook for 15-20 minutes, or until the peas are cooked through.

5. Remove the bouquet garni and serve.

TIME   Preparation takes about 25 minutes and cooking takes approximately 20 minutes.

VARIATION   Use whole new baby carrots when they are in season.

WATCHPOINT   Check the level of water during cooking and add more if the level has dropped.

SERVING TIP   Drain the peas, if preferred, before serving and add 15ml/1 tbsp of the cooking liquid to prevent them from being too dry.

☐

OPPOSITE

PETITS POIS A LA
FRANÇAISE

GLAZED VEGETABLES

*A springtime dish that is easy to prepare and cook,
and especially good served with grilled meats.*

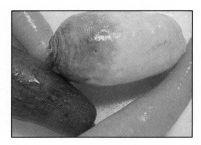

Step 1

Step 1

☐ 450g/1 lb carrots ☐ 1 large cucumber ☐ 450g/1 lb turnips
☐ 60g/4 tbsps butter ☐ 9 sugar cubes ☐ Salt and pepper

1. Wash and peel the vegetables as necessary. Cut them into long olive shapes with a sharp knife.

2. Melt the butter in a large frying pan and add the vegetables, salt, pepper and sugar. Stir, adding just enough water to cover the vegetables.

3. Cook over a high heat, allowing the water to evaporate.

4. Leave the vegetables to caramelise a little and then serve. Care should be taken as some vegetables cook more quickly than others. If time permits, cook the vegetables separately.

TIME   Preparation takes about 15 minutes and cooking takes approximately 30-45 minutes.

SERVING IDEAS   Cut the vegetables into different shapes, such as thin sticks or round slices.

WATCHPOINT   Should the vegetables cook before the water has completely evaporated, remove them, place the water over a high heat to reduce and then put the vegetables back to caramelise.

☐

OPPOSITE

GLAZED
VEGETABLES

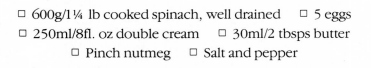

—— SERVES 6 ——

SPINACH FLANS

*Delicious individual spinach flans which
are rich and light at the same time.*

□ 600g/1¼ lb cooked spinach, well drained   □ 5 eggs
□ 250ml/8fl. oz double cream   □ 30ml/2 tbsps butter
□ Pinch nutmeg   □ Salt and pepper

1. Preheat the oven to 150°C/300°F/Gas Mark 2.

2. Squeeze out any excess water from the spinach with your fingers.

3. Add the eggs one by one to the chopped spinach, mixing well.

4. Add the cream, salt, pepper and nutmeg and mix well.

5. Grease 6 ramekin dishes with the butter, and spoon in the mixture.

6. Place the ramekins in a high-sided baking pan, pour in water to halfway up the sides and cook for approximately 40-50 minutes. Serve the flans hot.

TIME   Preparation takes about 20 minutes and cooking takes approximately 40 minutes.

VARIATION   Replace the spinach with sorrel or chard leaves.

WATCHPOINT   It is important to cook the flans in a bain marie, so that they cook gently without boiling.

□

OPPOSITE

SPINACH FLANS

——— SERVES 4 ———

MOULES MARINIERE

Mussels cooked in white wine: one of the best-known traditional French dishes.

Step 1

Step 1

Step 1

☐ 3 ltr/5 pints mussels, pre-soaked for 1 hour in salted water
☐ 1 large onion, thinly sliced   ☐ 2 cloves garlic, chopped
☐ 2 sprigs parsley, rinsed   ☐ 1 ltr/2 pints white wine
☐ 50g/2oz butter   ☐ Salt and pepper

TO SERVE

☐ 45ml/3 tbsps fresh parsley, chopped

1. Drain the mussels. Scrape off any persistent sand and rinse the mussels thoroughly in cold running water. Remove any stringy parts.

2. In a large saucepan, cook the mussels, onion, garlic, sprigs of parsley, half of the butter, salt and pepper for 4 minutes. Pour over the wine and cook for a further 8 minutes.

3. Take the saucepan off of the heat and remove the mussels with a slotted spoon. Allow them to cool a little and remove the mussels from the opened shells. Discard any that have not opened. Keep a few shells for decoration and discard the rest.

4. Keep the mussels warm.

5. Remove the sprigs of parsley from the cooking liquid and drain it through a fine sieve. Return the drained liquid to the saucepan over a high heat and bring to the boil. Allow to reduce by at least a third.

6. Stir in the remaining butter and a little more salt and pepper to taste. Stir in the mussels and the reserved shells. Serve hot.

TIME   The mussels need to be soaked for an hour. Preparation takes 5 minutes and cooking takes appoximately 35 minutes.

COOK'S TIP   Buy the smallest mussels you can find as they tend to have a richer flavour than the large variety.

TIME SAVER   The dish can be cooked in advance up to Step 6, and then reheated before serving, adding the remaining butter.

VARIATION   Stir 30ml/2 tbsps double cream into the sauce before serving.

☐

OPPOSITE

MOULES
MARINIERE

SERVES 6

BRANDADE DE MORUE

*This very rich and filling fish paste
needs to be begun a day in advance.*

Step 2

□ 1kg/2 ¼ lbs salt cod   □ 500ml/16fl. oz olive oil
□ 300ml/½ pint double cream
□ Pepper

---

1. Soak the salt cod for one day in cold water, changing the water frequently to remove the excess salt.

2. Poach the fish for 7 minutes on a high heat. Drain well. Remove all the bones and the skin, and flake the flesh very finely.

3. In a large saucepan, gently heat about 1/5 of the oil and add the fish, stirring well until a fine paste is reached.

4. Remove from the heat and, using a spatula, briskly work in the remaining oil and the cream, adding them alternately, drop by drop. Season well with pepper.

TIME   Preparation takes about 15 minutes, cooking takes 40 minutes and the soaking of the salt cod takes at least one day.

SERVING IDEA   Serve the brandade with small croutons rubbed with a clove of garlic and a little tomato sauce.

WATCHPOINT   When incorporating the oil and the cream it is important to work the mixture vigorously.

□

OPPOSITE

BRANDADE
DE MORUE

––––– SERVES 6 –––––

GRILLED TUNA STEAKS

*Delicious grilled tuna steaks make for great
barbeque food and are so much more sophisticated
than sausages or chops.*

Step 1

Step 1

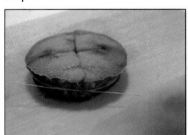

Step 1

□ 6 slices of fresh tuna   □ 30ml/2 tbsps herbes de Provence
□ 60ml/4 tbsps olive oil

TO SERVE

□ 1 tomato   □ 15ml/1 tbsp fresh herbs, chopped
□ 30ml/2 tbsp olive oil
□ 15ml/1 tbsp vinegar   □ Salt and pepper

1. Remove the bones from the tuna slices, roll the fish into rounds
and secure with kitchen string. Cut out the central bone and the
side bones from the slices of fish. Secure into rounds with kitchen
string.

2. Place on a shallow plate and pour over the olive oil.

3. Sprinkle over the herbes de Provence and place in the
refrigerator for at least 3 hours.

4. Preheat the griddle, frying pan or barbeque until very hot and
cook the fish until crispy on the outside and just slightly red in the
centre.

5. Peel the tomato and chop into small cubes.

6. Make a vinaigrette sauce by mixing together the vinegar, oil
and the herbs. Season well with salt and pepper. Stir in the tomato
and serve at the side of the fish.

TIME   Preparation takes about 15 minutes and marinating takes
at least 3 hours. Cooking takes about 15 minutes.

SERVING IDEA   Make up another measure of the tomato
vinaigrette sauce and serve it over a mixed salad.

WATCHPOINT   Should the steaks be very thick and you are
using a griddle or frying pan, just colour the fish under a high heat
and then finish cooking in the oven to avoid burning.

□

OPPOSITE

GRILLED TUNA
STEAKS

SERVES 6

BOW TIE SOLE FILLETS IN OYSTER SAUCE

With the rich flavour of oyster sauce, this is an imaginative way of serving sole – an ideal dinner party dish.

Step 1

Step 1

□ 3 sole fillets   □ 600ml/1 pint fish stock
□ 225g/8 oz mushrooms, rinsed, wiped and finely sliced
□ 12 oysters, shells removed   □ 2 tomatoes, wiped and diced
□ 45ml/3 tbsps double cream   □ Salt and pepper

---

1. Cut the sole fillets lengthwise into two and tie each piece into a knot, this makes the 'bow tie'.

2. In a large frying pan, cook the mushrooms and half of the tomatoes in the stock for 5 minutes.

3. Gently lower the 'bow ties' into the stock and cook gently for about 5 more minutes – cooking time will depend on the thickness of the fillets.

4. Carefully remove the cooked fillets with the help of a slotted spoon. Remove the sauce from the heat and stir in the cream.

5. Arrange the 'bow ties' neatly on a preheated serving dish.

6. Blend the sauce with a hand mixer until smooth. Stir the oysters into the sauce just prior to serving. Allow just enough time to heat the oysters through and pour immediately over the 'bow ties'. Sprinkle over the remaining diced tomato. Serve immediately.

TIME   Preparation takes about 10 minutes and total cooking time is about 30 minutes.

COOK'S TIP   Use the very best quality oysters on the market, they make all the difference to this dish. They should be firm, with not to much juice in the shell.

WATCHPOINT   The oysters should be cooked for a maximum of 2 minutes, otherwise they will shrink.

□

OPPOSITE

BOW TIE SOLE FILLETS IN OYSTER SAUCE

—— SERVES 6 ——

RED MULLET WITH CHIVES

*With its bright red fish and green sauce,
this dish is a certain eye-catcher*

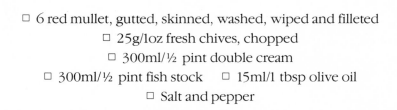

□ 6 red mullet, gutted, skinned, washed, wiped and filleted
□ 25g/1oz fresh chives, chopped
□ 300ml/½ pint double cream
□ 300ml/½ pint fish stock   □ 15ml/1 tbsp olive oil
□ Salt and pepper

1. Prepare the fish, making sure that all the bones have been removed.

2. In a saucepan over a brisk heat, reduce the fish stock by half, stir in the cream and reduce a little further. Stir in three-quarters of the chives and blend with a hand mixer until smooth.

3. Season the sauce with a little salt and pepper.

4. Heat the olive oil in a large frying pan and fry the mullet fillets until cooked through and slightly crisp.

5. Reheat the sauce, but do not allow it to boil.

6. Serve the fillets on a bed of the sauce.

Step 1

TIME   Preparation takes 5 minutes and cooking takes about 25 minutes.

SERVING IDEA   Garnish the dish with fresh chives.

Step 4

□

OPPOSITE

RED MULLET
WITH CHIVES

——— SERVES 6 ———

ROLLED SOLE FILLETS

*An absolute delight to the eye and palate, these delicate
sole rolls, with their herb stuffing and mushroom sauce,
are sure winners every time.*

Step 1

Step 2

Step 2

☐ 12 small sole fillets
☐ 30ml/2 tbsps fresh herbs, chopped (parsley, chive, basil etc.)
☐ 600ml/1 pint fish stock   ☐ 300ml/½ pint double cream
☐ 225g/8oz mushrooms, rinsed, wiped and chopped
☐ 1 clove garlic, chopped   ☐ Salt and pepper

1. Beat the sole fillets flat, between 2 sheets of cling film, with light strokes of a rolling pin.

2. Sprinkle the fresh herbs over the fish and then roll up the fillets.

3. In a saucepan over a high heat, boil the stock and allow to reduce by half. Add the mushrooms and garlic and cook for a further 8 minutes. Remove from the heat, beat in the cream and add a little salt and pepper. Remove the mushrooms and set them aside for Step 6.

4. Remove the saucepan from the heat and allow the stock to cool a little. Blend until smooth in a blender.

5. Meanwhile, steam the fish rolls until cooked – approximately 8 minutes.

6. Replace the mushrooms and reheat the sauce, but do not let it boil.

7. Serve the sole rolls on a warmed serving dish with the sauce poured over.

TIME   It takes about 15 minutes to prepare all the ingredients. Cooking takes about 30 minutes.

COOK'S TIP   The fillets can be gently tied with fine kitchen string at the end of Step 2 – this will help them to keep their shape whilst cooking. Do not forget to remove the strings before serving.

MICROWAVE TIP   The fish can be prepared in advance and reheated in the microwave before serving.

WATCHPOINT   The sauce should be made just prior to serving. Do not allow it to boil.

☐

OPPOSITE

ROLLED
SOLE FILLETS

GRILLED TROUT

A quick and easy recipe for trout, this is one of the most popular ways of serving this fish in France.

Step 1

Step 1

□ 6 river trout, gutted, washed and wiped
□ 30ml/2 tbsps olive oil □ 125ml/5fl. oz fresh fish roe
□ Juice of 1 lemon □ Salt and pepper

1. Begin by preparing the trout. Cut off their fins, scale them, gut them, wash well under running water and dry them on paper towels.

2. If using a grill, set it to high, or heat up a flat griddle or frying pan.

3. Dip the trout in the olive oil and sprinkle them with salt and pepper. Cook the fish until nicely marked on the outside and just tender on the inside.

4. Pour a little lemon juice on each fish and serve hot with a spoonful of fish roe on the top.

TIME   It will take about 10 minutes to prepare the fish and approximately 20 minutes to cook them, depending on their thickness.

SERVING IDEA   If you are serving the trout for a dinner party, use caviar instead of ordinary roe, omitting the salt in Step 3.

COOK'S TIP   If using a traditional flat griddle, heat it until very hot and mark the fish by searing first in one direction and then turning the fish 90° and searing again. You can then finish cooking in a moderate oven.

□

OPPOSITE

GRILLED TROUT

—— SERVES 6 ——

CRAB SALAD WITH RUM

A lovely light salad to make when fresh crab is available.
The dish can also be made with canned crab meat.

□ 1 large can crab meat, drained □ 2 avocados
□ 4 artichoke hearts
□ 1 head lettuce, washed, dried and shredded
□ 3 sticks celery, wiped, strings removed and diced
□ Juice of 2 lemons

SAUCE

□ 1 egg yolk □ 150ml/¼ pint oil □ 10ml/2 tsps mustard
□ 60ml/4 tbsps single cream □ 15ml/1 tbsp chopped parsley
□ A jigger of rum □ Salt and pepper

Step 3

1. Have the lemon juice ready. Peel the avocado pears and, with a melon baller, scoop out the flesh. Dip the balls immediately into the lemon juice, then place them in a bowl in the refrigerator.

2. Dice the artichoke hearts and dip them into the lemon juice. Put them in the refrigerator with the avocado balls.

3. Make the sauce by beating the egg yolk with the mustard. Beat in the oil, drop by drop, then beat in the cream, rum, parsley, salt and pepper.

4. Place a small bed of lettuce on 6 individual plates, and top with the avocado, artichoke and the diced celery. Break up the crab meat and scatter over the salad.

5. Serve with the rum sauce dotted over.

Step 3

TIME   Preparation takes about 30 minutes.

SERVING IDEA   If time and budget permit, use fresh crab cooked in fish stock.

WATCHPOINT   Do not cut the avocado or the artichoke too far in advance of serving, as even with the lemon juice they tend to discolour.

□

OPPOSITE

CRAB SALAD
WITH RUM

─── SERVES 6-8 ───

MARINATED HERRINGS

A dish to prepare in advance and serve on warm summer evenings, or perhaps on picnics.

Step 1

Step 1

☐ 1 ltr/2 pints olive oil   ☐ 6 smoked herrings, cut into small fillets
☐ 2 onions, sliced   ☐ 6 bay leaves
☐ 1 carrot, scraped and thinly sliced   ☐ 10 coriander seeds

1. Put half the onion, coriander, bay leaves and carrot in a terrine. Interleave the herring fillets among them. Cover with the remaining half of the vegetables and herbs and pour the olive oil over.

2. Leave to marinate in a cool place for at least 2 days.

3. Serve either directly from the terrine, or cut into smaller pieces on individual plates. Add a slice of tomato and a few leaves of salad and spoon over a little of the marinade.

TIME   Preparation takes about 20 minutes, plus at least 2 days marinating time.

VARIATION   The addition of fresh herbs, such as parsley or chives, adds not only colour but a distinctive flavour as well.

SERVING IDEAS   Serve with crisp French stick with lots of butter.

COOK'S TIP   This dish can be made up to 2 weeks in advance and kept in the fridge.

☐

OPPOSITE

MARINATED
HERRINGS

COD WITH LEEKS

*Large slices of cod are required for this dish. Keep the
skin on the fish for an attractive presentation.*

Step 1

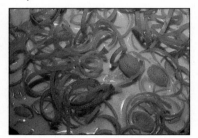

Step 2

Step 3

□ 900g/2lbs leeks, well rinsed and drained
□ 2 thick pieces of cod   □ 450ml/¾ pint single cream
□ Salt and pepper   □ 15ml/1 tbsp fresh chives, chopped

---

1. Cut each piece of cod into two, removing any bones. Sprinkle with salt and pepper and keep in a cool place.

2. Cut the leeks into very fine slices, put them in a frying pan and pour over the cream. Cook on a very gentle heat for 10 minutes, covered.

3. Add the fish to the leeks and continue cooking for 10 minutes.

4. Serve the leek and cream base on a pre-heated plate with the fillets placed on top and the chives sprinkled over.

TIME   Preparation takes about 5 minutes, and cooking takes 20 minutes.

WATCHPOINT   Check during cooking that the cream has not evaporated too quickly. If this should be the case add a little more cream.

VARIATION   This dish can be prepared with other types of fish if cod is not available

□

OPPOSITE

COD WITH LEEKS

CALAMARS DE PROVENCE

A traditional recipe for squid from the South of France.

Step 1

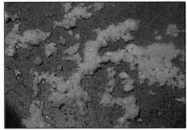

Step 2

Step 2

Step 3

□

OPPOSITE

CALAMARS
DE PROVENCE

□ 2.5kg/5 ½ lbs squid, washed and cut into thin slices
□ 5 onions, chopped   □ 5 cloves garlic, chopped
□ 5 tomatoes, chopped   □ 250ml/8fl. oz white wine
□ 250ml/8fl. oz fish stock   □ 15ml/1 tbsp double cream
□ 1 pinch saffron   □ 15ml/1 tbsp olive oil
□ 5ml/1 tsp cayenne pepper   □ 1 bouquet garni
□ 5ml/1 tsp fennel seeds (optional)   □ Salt and pepper

1. Warm the oil in a frying pan and cook the squid and fennel seeds until all the juices evaporate.

2. Remove the squid and add the onion, garlic, cayenne pepper, bouquet garni and the tomatoes. Stir well and cook for a few minutes.

3. Pour over the stock and the wine, sprinkle over the saffron, and stir well. Cook on a fairly brisk heat until the sauce has reduced somewhat. Return the squid to the pan.

4. Reduce the heat, cover and cook very gently until the squid is tender.

5. Just before serving, remove the bouquet garni and stir in the cream. Check the seasoning and add a little salt and pepper if necessary.

TIME   Preparation takes about 25 minutes and cooking takes approximately 40 minutes.

WATCHPOINT   Should the cream separate when you add it to the sauce, pour the sauce into a blender, add some single cream and blend until smooth.

SERVING IDEA   Serve with whole brown rice or Rice Pilaf.

—— SERVES 6 ——

SLICED CHICKEN
WITH FIGS

*A new recipe that presents chicken in a new light –
this recipe will delight all who taste it.*

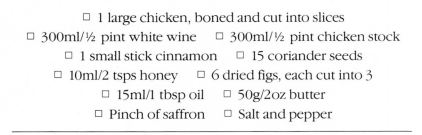

□ 1 large chicken, boned and cut into slices
□ 300ml/½ pint white wine □ 300ml/½ pint chicken stock
□ 1 small stick cinnamon □ 15 coriander seeds
□ 10ml/2 tsps honey □ 6 dried figs, each cut into 3
□ 15ml/1 tbsp oil □ 50g/2oz butter
□ Pinch of saffron □ Salt and pepper

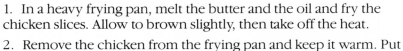

1. In a heavy frying pan, melt the butter and the oil and fry the chicken slices. Allow to brown slightly, then take off the heat.

2. Remove the chicken from the frying pan and keep it warm. Put the frying pan back on the heat and add the cinnamon, wine, stock, saffron, coriander, figs, honey, salt and pepper. Stir well and cook for 4 minutes. Return the chicken to the frying pan, cover, and continue cooking for 20 minutes on a very gentle heat.

3. Remove the chicken and the figs and keep them warm.

4. Remove and discard the cinnamon.

5. Allow the sauce to boil until quite syrupy.

6. Return the chicken and the figs to the frying pan, heat through and serve.

TIME   Preparation takes about 5 minutes and cooking takes about 35 minutes.

SERVING IDEA   Serve with Rice Pilaf.

WATCHPOINT   Cook over a very gentle heat throughout Step 2, stirring from time to time to prevent sticking.

©Copyright F. Lebain.

□

OPPOSITE

SLICED CHICKEN
WITH FIGS

SERVES 6

LAPIN CHASSEUR

*'Hunter's rabbit,' a delicious blend of mushrooms,
smoked bacon and white wine, all cooked on top of
the stove in less than an hour.*

Step 1

Step 2

Step 2

Step 3

□ 1 rabbit   □ 1 onion, chopped   □ 1 bouquet garni
□ 300ml/½ pint white wine
□ 300g/12 oz button mushrooms, sliced
□ 100g/4 oz smoked bacon, diced   □ 15ml/1 tbsp flour
□ 15ml/1 tbsp butter   □ 15ml/1 tbsp parsley, chopped
□ Pinch nutmeg   □ Salt and pepper

1. Bone the rabbit and cut the meat into small pieces.

2. Cook the bacon in a casserole on the top of the stove without adding any extra fat, until the fat from the bacon is running. Stir in the rabbit pieces, add the onions and continue cooking until the onions are tender.

3. Pour over the wine and 300ml/½ pint water. Add the bouquet garni, nutmeg, salt and pepper. Bring to the boil.

4. Cover, reduce the heat and cook for 30 minutes. Add the mushrooms and then simmer gently for a further 15 minutes.

5. Just before serving, beat together the butter and the flour. Mix this into the sauce, off of the heat, little by little until the sauce thickens to the desired consistency.

6. Serve with the parsley sprinkled over.

TIME   Preparation takes about 15 minutes and cooking takes approximately 45 minutes.

SERVING IDEA   Serve with fresh wild mushrooms gently sautéed in butter and garlic.

WATCHPOINT   When adding flour and butter at step 5, take care that the sauce does not thicken too much or too quickly.

□

OPPOSITE

LAPIN CHASSEUR

——— SERVES 6 ———

CHICKEN WITH
TARRAGON SAUCE

Tarragon is a much used herb in the French kitchen. In this recipe, it adds its very distinctive flavour to the rich sauce.

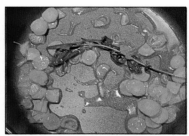

Step 2

Step 3

Step 5

☐ 2 chickens, chopped into pieces ☐ 6 shallots, chopped
☐ 1 carrot, chopped ☐ 30ml/2 tbsps fresh tarragon, chopped
☐ 3 sprigs fresh tarragon ☐ 45ml/3 tbsps olive oil
☐ 100g/4oz butter
☐ 1 sherry glass Muscat ☐ 150ml/¼ pint white wine
☐ 300ml/½ pint chicken stock ☐ Salt and pepper
☐ 15ml/1 tbsp cornflour mixed with 15ml/1 tbsp water

1. Warm the oil and half of the butter in a large casserole and brown the chicken pieces on all sides. Remove the chicken to a spare plate.

2. Add the remaining butter to the casserole and cook the shallots, carrot and the sprigs of tarragon for 5 minutes.

3. Slide the chicken pieces back into the casserole and stir well.

4. Stir in the Muscat.

5. Pour over the wine and the chicken stock, add salt and pepper, and stir well. Bring to the boil, cover, then reduce the heat and simmer for 30 minutes. Check the level of the juices and add a little water if necessary.

6. When the chicken pieces are cooked through, remove and place on a preheated serving dish.

7. Bring the sauce to the boil and allow to reduce and thicken. If necessary, stir in the cornflour and water mixture, stirring continuously until the sauce has thickened. Serve poured over the chicken. Sprinkle over the chopped tarragon.

TIME   Preparation will take about 15 minutes and cooking takes about 40 minutes.

SERVING IDEA   Serve with sauté potatoes and garnish with sprigs of tarragon.

COOK'S TIP   If time permits, allow the sauce to reduce and thicken by itself. Only use the cornflour if the sauce is really too thin.

☐

OPPOSITE

CHICKEN WITH
TARRAGON SAUCE

DUCK BREAST WITH GREEN PEPPERCORN SAUCE

*Duck is an ever-popular dish in France, served here
in a highly flavoured, rich pepper sauce.*

Step 3

Step 5

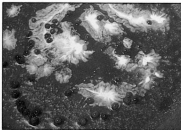

Step 5

☐ 3 large duck breasts
☐ 1kg/2¼ lbs duck or poultry bones and trimmings
☐ 15ml/1 tbsp green peppercorns
☐ 1 onion, finely chopped ☐ 1 carrot, finely chopped
☐ 1 leek, finely chopped ☐ 300ml/½ pint white wine
☐ 15ml/1 tbsp Cognac ☐ 15ml/1 tbsp oil
☐ 200ml/6 fl. oz double cream ☐ 5ml/1 tsp thyme
☐ 1 bay leaf ☐ Salt and pepper

1. Break up the bones and cook them in the oil in a heavy frying pan with the trimmings, 30ml/2 tbsps water, onion, carrot and leek for 5 minutes. Pour over the white wine and enough water to cover. Add salt and pepper, thyme and bay leaf, bring to the boil and allow to reduce by half.

2. When the sauce has reduced, strain it through a fine sieve, return to the heat and reduce a little more.

3. Score the skin of the duck breasts and, in a clean frying pan, seal over a high heat, skin side first. Once sealed on all sides, continue cooking in a hot oven until just a thin line of pink is visible in the centre – approximately 10 to 15 minutes.

4. Set the breasts aside and keep them warm.

5. Sauté the peppercorns in the fat from the sealed duck breasts for 1 minute, add the Cognac, then stir in the reduced sauce from Step 2. Allow this to reduce a little more and then stir in the cream.

6. Cut the breasts into even slices and serve with the sauce poured over.

TIME   Preparation takes about 5 minutes and cooking takes about 40 minutes.

VARIATION   You could use duck fillets instead of breasts.

COOK'S TIP   Ask your butcher to put by the bones and trimmings a few days prior to your buying the fillets; they are essential for the rich flavouring of the sauce.

WATCHPOINT   If you prefer your meat well cooked, give the breasts a little extra time in the oven. Find out how your guests prefer their meat cooked prior to serving.

☐

OPPOSITE

DUCK BREAST
WITH GREEN
PEPPERCORN
SAUCE

—— SERVES 6 ——

PERDREAUX A L'ARMAGNAC

Young, plump and tender partridges are ideal for this classic recipe. Fresh truffles are now available in specialist shops; they are expensive, but for a special meal well worth the extra cost.

Step 1

☐ 3 young partridges, cleaned, gizzards and the livers removed and retained ☐ 1 truffle
☐ 100ml/4fl. oz double cream ☐ 60ml/4 tbsps Armagnac
☐ 50g/2oz butter ☐ 15ml/1 tbsp oil

1. Truss the birds with kitchen string. Melt ⅓ of the butter with the oil in a heavy saucepan and brown the birds on all sides. Remove them from the saucepan (retain the saucepan with the juices) and cook in a hot oven for 20 minutes.

2. Once the birds are cooked, cut off the wings, thighs and the breasts, set them aside and keep warm.

3. Crush the carcasses and put them back into the saucepan containing the juices and add the gizzards and livers. Over a high heat, pour over the Armagnac and the cream and stir well. Take off the heat and strain through a fine sieve.

4. Add the crumbled truffle and whip in the remaining butter. Blend in a mixer or food processor until smooth.

5. Cut the partridges into slices and serve the sauce poured over.

TIME   Preparation takes about 10 minutes and cooking takes about 30 minutes.

VARIATION   If partridge is unavailable, use wood pigeon instead.

☐

OPPOSITE

PERDREAUX A
L'ARMAGNAC

FILLET OF LAMB WITH FRESH THYME SAUCE

A delicately flavoured sauce to go with tender spring lamb, filleted from the saddle.

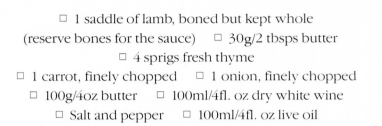

□ 1 saddle of lamb, boned but kept whole
(reserve bones for the sauce)   □ 30g/2 tbsps butter
□ 4 sprigs fresh thyme
□ 1 carrot, finely chopped   □ 1 onion, finely chopped
□ 100g/4oz butter   □ 100ml/4fl. oz dry white wine
□ Salt and pepper   □ 100ml/4fl. oz live oil

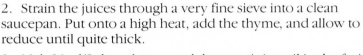

1. Heat half of the olive oil and sauté the broken bones with the carrot and onion. Wipe out any excess fat, deglaze the frying pan with the wine, cover the ingredients with water and leave at a gentle boil for 1 hour.

2. Strain the juices through a very fine sieve into a clean saucepan. Put onto a high heat, add the thyme, and allow to reduce until quite thick.

3. Melt 30ml/2 tbsps butter and the remaining oil in the frying pan and seal the lamb on all sides. Finish cooking the lamb in a hot oven for 15 minutes.

4. Just before serving, strain the reduced juices through a fine sieve to eliminate the thyme. Mix the remaining 100g/4oz butter into the sauce, and blend smooth with a hand mixer. Cut the lamb into slices and serve.

TIME   Preparation will take about 10 minutes, longer if you are boning the meat yourself. Cooking takes approximately 1 hour and 30 minutes.

SERVING IDEA   Serve with a Gratin Dauphinois.

COOK'S TIP   If the rolled fillet is very thick and you like your lamb well cooked, cook the lamb for longer in the oven at the end of Step 3.

□

OPPOSITE

FILLET OF LAMB
WITH FRESH
THYME SAUCE

CALF'S LIVER
WITH ORANGE SAUCE

*Serve this delicious recipe with confidence for your most
elegant dinner parties; it's sure to be a great success.*

Step 1

Step 2

☐ 1 large piece of calf's liver, cut into slices
☐ 4 oranges (2 squeezed for their juice, and the remaining
2 peeled and cut into thin slices)
☐ 300ml/½ pint veal stock   ☐ 80g/3oz butter
☐ Salt and pepper   ☐ 15ml/1 tbsp chopped chives

1. Heat ¾ of the butter in a frying pan and cook the liver briskly
on both sides. Remove the liver and keep warm on a plate over a
saucepan of boiling water.

2. Wipe out the excess fat, deglaze the pan with the juice of 2
oranges and scrape the bottom of the pan with a wooden spoon
to mix any remaining liver into the juice. Add the veal stock, salt
and pepper, bring to the boil and add the orange slices.

3. Allow to colour slightly, remove the slices with a fork and place
them on the liver.

4. Remove the pan from the heat and stir in the remaining butter.

5. Serve the sauce poured over the liver and sliced oranges.
Garnish with the chopped chives.

TIME   Preparation takes about 8 minutes and cooking takes
approximately 25 to 30 minutes.

SERVING IDEA   Serve with boiled or steamed new potatoes.

VARIATION   Replace 2 of the oranges with a large grapefruit.
Cut it in half, squeeze the juice from one half and peel and slice
the remaining half. Divide 2 oranges in the same way.

☐

OPPOSITE

CALF'S LIVER WITH
ORANGE SAUCE

SERVES 4

STEAMED CALVES' LIVER

*A richly flavoured sauce with fresh tarragon
enhances the calves' liver delightfully;
the liver should be served slightly pink.*

Step 1

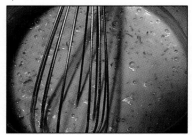

Step 4

☐ 1kg/2 ¼ lbs calves' liver ☐ 1 sprig fresh tarragon
☐ 2 shallots, chopped
☐ 5ml/1 tsp peppercorns, lightly crushed
☐ 90ml/6 tbsps vinegar
☐ 300ml/½ pint whipping cream, whipped
☐ 90ml/6 tbsps butter ☐ 90ml/6 tbsps milk
☐ Salt and pepper

1. Chop half of the tarragon finely and put it into a saucepan with the vinegar, shallots and peppercorns. Heat, and allow to boil until the vinegar has almost completely evaporated, then whip in the cream and the milk. Allow to reduce and then strain through a fine sieve. Remove from the heat, but keep warm.

2. Steam the liver on a bed of the remaining tarragon until still just pink in the centre. Sprinkle with salt and pepper.

3. Slice the liver thinly and serve on a pre-heated plate.

4. Put the sauce back onto a gentle heat and whisk in the butter. Serve the sauce immediately.

TIME Preparation takes about 5 minutes and cooking takes 40 minutes.

WATCHPOINT Serve the sauce immediately and do not try to reheat it once the butter has been added.

COOK'S TIP Find out in advance how guests prefer their liver cooked.

WATCHPOINT Be careful when reducing the sauce during Step 1; it thickens very quickly, and you must remove the sauce from the heat before it becomes too thick.

☐

OPPOSITE

STEAMED CALVES'
LIVER

—————— SERVES 6 ——————

CASSOULET

*A classic casserole, served throughout France. Great
for cold winter evenings in front of a roaring fire.*

Step 1

Step 1

Step 2

Step 2

□
OPPOSITE

CASSOULET

□ 1.5kg/3 ½ lbs broad beans, presoaked (12 hours)   □ 1 onion
□ 2 whole cloves   □ 1 leek, cut into chunks
□ 1 carrot, cut into chunks   □ 700g/1 ½ lbs pork loin
□ 100g/4oz goose or other poultry dripping
□ 2 cloves garlic, chopped   □ 1 pork knuckle
□ 300g/¾ lb bacon, whole   □ ½ shoulder lamb
225g/½ lb herb sausages   □ 4 tomatoes, halved
□ 1 bouquet garni
□ 5ml/1 tsp thyme   □ 1 bay leaf   □ Salt and pepper

1. In a large flameproof casserole, melt the dripping and seal the pork knuckle and the loin. Then add the onion, garlic, leek, tomatoes, carrot, bay leaf and the bouquet garni. Stir well and cook for a few minutes.

2. Add the drained beans, and enough water to cover the contents of the casserole. Bring to the boil then reduce the heat, cover and simmer for 2 hours on a very gentle heat. After about one hour, add the sausages, bacon, and the shoulder of lamb. Check the water level during cooking and add water when necessary.

3. After the full 2 hours, strain off the juice into a clean saucepan and chop the meat into bite-sized pieces. Discard most of the bones.

4. Remove the bay leaf and the bouquet garni.

5. In a large earthenware bowl, place layers of the chopped meats, beans and sausages. Pour over 600 – 900ml/1 – 1 ½ pints of the cooking juice, cover and continue cooking in a hot oven for 35 minutes.

6. Serve piping hot from the oven.

TIME   Preparation takes about 20 minutes and cooking takes approximately 3 hours.

COOK'S TIP   Cassoulet is even better if cooked the day before and reheated just before serving. Make sure that there is enough liquid in the casserole, adding water as necessary.

SERVING IDEA   Simply serve plenty of French bread with this substantial main course.

----- SERVES 6 -----

KIDNEY FRICASSEE

Sautéed calf's kidney in a sweet, creamy sauce.

- □ 900g/2 lbs calf's kidney □ 250g/9oz mushrooms, sliced
- □ 30ml/2 tbsps Madeira □ 200ml/6fl. oz veal stock
- □ 100ml/3 ½ fl. oz double cream □ 15ml/1 tbsp olive oil
- □ Salt and pepper

1. Prepare the kidney by cutting it into small cubes. Heat the oil in a frying pan and sauté the kidney and the mushrooms. Season with salt and pepper. Remove the kidney and keep it warm.

2. Deglaze the frying pan with the Madeira and allow the liquid to reduce a little. Stir in the stock and reduce by half.

3. Stir in the cream and add the salt and pepper. Put the kidney back into the sauce and heat through. Serve hot.

TIME   Preparation takes about 15 minutes and cooking takes approximately 30 minutes.

COOK'S TIP   You will notice that the cooked kidney loses a lot of blood once you have removed it from the frying pan. Allow this blood to drain off – do not add it to the sauce.

□

OPPOSITE

KIDNEY FRICASSEE

SERVES 4

SAUTE D'AGNEAU

A quick and easy recipe consisting of tender lamb in red wine and mushroom sauce, all done on the top of a stove.

Step 1

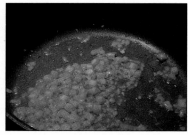

Step 2

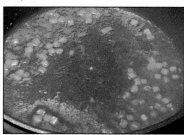

Step 3

Step 4

□ 1kg/2 ¼ lbs shoulder of lamb, cut into chunks
□ 30ml/2 tbsps olive oil □ 3 sticks celery, cut into small cubes
□ 1 onion, finely chopped □ 175ml/6fl. oz red wine
□ 175ml/6fl. oz beef stock
□ 30ml/2 tbsps cornflour mixed with 30ml/2 tbsps water
□ 15ml/1 tbsp tomato purée
□ 225g/8oz mushrooms, washed, wiped and sliced
□ Salt and pepper

1. Warm half the olive oil in a frying pan and seal the pieces of lamb on all sides. Allow to brown slightly, then remove from the heat and keep warm.

2. Add the remaining oil and sauté the celery, onion and mushrooms.

3. Stirring constantly, add the wine, stock, tomato purée and the dissolved cornflour. Stir until the sauce thickens.

4. Put the lamb back in the frying pan with the above ingredients, add a little salt and pepper, cover and cook for a further 15 to 25 minutes.

5. Remove the lamb and blend the sauce in a blender until smooth. Serve the meat with the sauce poured over.

TIME   Preparation takes about 5 minutes and cooking time is approximately 40 minutes.

ECONOMY   Remove a few pieces of celery before blending the sauce; these will serve as a ready-made garnish.

SERVING IDEA   Serve with boiled or steamed new potatoes.

□

OPPOSITE

SAUTE D'AGNEAU

SERVES 6

ROAST PORK WITH
GARLIC CREAM

*A distinctively-flavoured sauce enhances the roast pork
marvellously in a dish that is definitely for garlic lovers.*

Step 1

Step 1

▢ 1kg/2 ¼ lb pork roast   ▢ 1 head garlic, all the cloves peeled
▢ 300ml/½ pint single cream, whipped
▢ 30ml/2 tbsps oil   ▢ 100ml/3 ½ fl. oz port
▢ 1 knob butter   ▢ Salt and pepper

---

1. Trim off any excess fat or gristle from the meat, setting the trimmings aside for use in the sauce, roll the meat into a roast and secure with string.

2. Sauté the meat trimmings in half of the oil with the garlic, and allow to brown slightly. Pour off the excess fat from the pan and stir in the port. Remove from the heat and stir in the cream.

3. Remove a few cloves of garlic for decoration. Blend the sauce smooth with a hand mixer and then strain through a fine sieve.

4. Put the sauce back on the heat and allow to reduce a little. Remove from the heat and keep it warm.

5. Warm the remaining oil in a large frying pan and seal the roast on all sides. Finish cooking in a moderately hot oven for 20 to 40 minutes depending on the thickness of the roast.

6. Slice the roast and serve on a pre-heated plate with the sauce poured over and the few cloves of garlic as decoration.

TIME   Preparation will take about 15 minutes and cooking takes about 1 hour.

SERVING IDEA   Serve with a colourful vegetable such as carrot or broccoli.

COOK'S TIP   When sealing the meat, allow it to brown nicely, making the finished dish even more appetizing.

WATCHPOINT   To help keep the meat moist, wrap the roast in aluminium foil halfway through the oven cooking time.

▢

OPPOSITE

ROAST PORK WITH
GARLIC CREAM

PAUPIETTES DE VEAU

Veal paupiettes or birds are a delicious way of serving this lean, delicate and distinctive tasting meat.

Step 3

Step 3

Step 3

☐

OPPOSITE

PAUPIETTES DE
VEAU

☐ 6 very thin slices of veal, each weighing approximately 100g/4oz
☐ 150g/6oz shoulder veal   ☐ 1 egg   ☐ 50g/2oz butter
☐ 4 sprigs parsley   ☐ 3 shallots, finely chopped
☐ 2 onions, finely chopped   ☐ 4 tomatoes, halved
☐ 3 button mushrooms   ☐ Bouquet garni
☐ 1 sherry glass port   ☐ 150ml/¼ pint double cream
☐ Salt and pepper

1. Trim the slices of veal into even-sized rectangles. Keep the veal in a cool place whilst making the stuffing.

2. Mince the trimmings, shoulder of veal, parsley, mushrooms, salt and pepper together in a food processor.

3. Beat the egg with 15ml/1 tbsp cream and mix this egg mixture and the minced meat together well. Place the stuffing on the slices of veal and roll them up into neat oblongs. Tie with kitchen string.

4. Melt half of the butter in a frying pan and seal the veal on all sides until nicely browned. Continue cooking for approximately 10 minutes.

5. Pour over the port, stir, and add the tomatoes, shallots, bouquet garni and a little more pepper. Cover, and leave to simmer gently for 30 minutes.

6. To serve, place the paupiettes on a pre-heated serving dish. Remove the bouquet garni from the sauce, stir the remaining cream into the sauce and pour over the paupiettes. If you prefer a smooth sauce, strain it through a fine sieve and then blend smooth with a hand mixer.

TIME   Preparation takes about 30 minutes and cooking takes approximately 50 minutes.

SERVING IDEA   Remove the string from the paupiettes and cut each one into slices.

GARNISH   Garnish the dish with a little chopped carrot and parsley.

WATCHPOINT   Do not allow the sauce to boil once you have stirred in the remaining cream.

—— SERVES 6 ——

MIGNON DE PORC AU CHOU

Pork fillet, roasted with cabbage and bacon.

Step 1

Step 2

Step 4

☐ 1kg/2 ¼ lbs pork fillet, cut in two
☐ 225g/½ lb smoked bacon, chopped   ☐ 100g/4oz drippings
☐ 1kg/2 ¼ lbs green cabbage, shredded
☐ 300ml/½ pint chicken stock   ☐ Salt and pepper

1. Remove any gristle from the meat and cut off any excess fat. Roll up the roasts and tie them securely with kitchen string.

2. Bring to the boil a large quantity of lightly salted water and blanch the shredded cabbage for 2 minutes. Drain well, squeezing out excess water.

3. Melt the drippings in a large frying pan and seal the pork on all sides. Allow the meat to brown slightly, then remove the roasts and keep them warm.

4. Add the bacon and cabbage to the frying pan, stir well, and cook for 4 minutes.

5. Transfer the contents to a casserole, add the roasts and the stock, and finish cooking in a moderately hot oven for approximately 40 minutes.

6. Turn the cabbage, juices and roasts from time to time in the oven. When cooked, cut the roasts into slices and serve hot.

TIME   Preparation takes about 15 minutes and cooking takes approximately 1 hour.

WATCHPOINT   When turning the contents of the casserole, make sure that the meat is well covered with the juice and cabbage otherwise it will be too dry. Add a little more stock if the liquid evaporates too quickly.

SERVING IDEA   Serve with roast potatoes.

VARIATION   Use pork chops instead of fillet.

☐

OPPOSITE

MIGNON DE PORC
AU CHOU

SERVES 6

CARRE D'AGNEAU A LA PROVENÇALE

Herbes de Provence, a mixture of dried herbs with a dominance of thyme, give this rack of lamb recipe from the South of France a distinctive flavour.

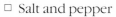

☐ 2 racks lamb (6 to 8 chops per rack)
☐ 15ml/1 tbsp herbes de Provence
☐ 1 clove garlic, finely chopped
☐ 15ml/1 tbsp fresh parsley, chopped ☐ 45ml/3 tbsps olive oil
☐ Salt and pepper

1. Begin the night before by preparing the oil. In a large screw-top jar, mix together the oil, parsley, garlic, herbs, salt and lots of pepper. Shake well.

2. Make small incisions all over the lamb and pour over the oil, basting the meat with the oil several times.

3. The next day, preheat the oven to 200°C/400°F/Gas Mark 6 and cook the lamb for approximately 15 minutes, slightly longer if you prefer your meat a little less pink.

TIME   Preparation takes about 5 minutes, with overnight mixing for the oil, and about 20 to 30 minutes cooking.

SERVING IDEA   Serve with Haricots Verts à la Provencale.

COOK'S TIP   Choose a rack of lamb with long, thin chops, as this will cook more quickly.

☐

OPPOSITE

CARRE D'AGNEAU A
LA PROVENÇALE

—— SERVES 6 ——

ESTOUFFADE DE BOEUF

*A rich beef casserole with olives and mushrooms
– perfect as a warming winter dinner.*

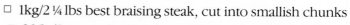

- □ 1kg/2 ¼ lbs best braising steak, cut into smallish chunks
- □ 225g/8oz smoked bacon, cubed   □ 4 onions, sliced
- □ 2 cloves garlic, chopped   □ 1 bottle red wine
- □ 150g/6oz mushrooms, sliced   □ 100g/4oz pitted black olives
- □ 30ml/2 tbsps olive oil   □ 30ml/2 tbsps plain flour
- □ 1 bouquet garni (with lots of thyme)   □ Salt and pepper

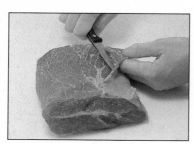

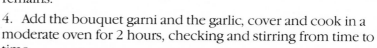

1. Heat 15ml/1 tbsp olive oil in a large, flame-proof casserole and cook the bacon until the juices run.

2. Roll the meat in the flour and shake off the excess. Add the meat to the casserole with the bacon and the onions and seal the meat on all sides. Wipe out the excess fat.

3. Add salt and pepper and pour over the wine. Stir well, then allow to reduce over a high heat, until about half of the liquid remains.

4. Add the bouquet garni and the garlic, cover and cook in a moderate oven for 2 hours, checking and stirring from time to time.

5. Sauté the mushrooms in the remaining olive oil.

6. Strain the contents of the casserole through a sieve, catching the juices in a clean saucepan. Put the meat and onions back into the casserole and add the sautéed mushrooms.

7. Put the juices back on the heat, skim off any rising fat, then stir in the olives.

8. Pour this sauce back over the contents of the casserole and cook for a further 20 minutes. Remove the bouquet garni. Serve hot.

TIME   Preparation will take about 10 minutes and cooking takes approximately 1 hour and 40 minutes.

COOK'S TIP   The estouffade is even more delicious if reheated and served the following day.

SERVING IDEA   Serve with boiled or steamed new potatoes.

WINE TIP   Serve the same wine as you have used in the cooking of the dish.

□

OPPOSITE

ESTOUFFADE
DE BOEUF

—————— SERVES 6 ——————

BEEF BOURGUIGNON

*A great French classic, this traditional beef
casserole should be cooked using a very good
claret to give it its extremely rich flavour.*

Step 2

Step 2

Step 2

☐ 2kg/4 ½ lbs braising steak, cut into cubes
☐ 6 rashers smoked bacon, cut into small pieces
☐ 20 baby onions, peeled
☐ 30ml/2 tbsps flour   ☐ 15ml/1 tbsp oil
☐ A bottle of red wine   ☐ Salt and pepper

1. In a large saucepan, cook the bacon and the onions without adding any extra fat. Remove with a slotted spoon once they begin to brown.

2. Add the oil and seal the cubes of meat on all sides. Sprinkle over the flour, allow it to brown slightly and pour over the wine, stirring well. Add water to cover only if necessary. Add salt and pepper and bring to the boil.

3. Reduce the heat and replace the onions and the bacon from Step 1. Cover and simmer for 2 hours.

4. Serve hot.

TIME   Preparation takes about 5 minutes and cooking takes 2 hours and 10 minutes.

SERVING IDEA   Delicious with boiled baby carrots and new potatoes. Serve with a bottle of the same wine used for cooking.

COOK'S TIP   Simmer on a very, very gentle heat for at least 2 hours. Watch the level of the juices and add a little water, if necessary, during cooking.

☐

OPPOSITE

BEEF
BOURGUIGNON

———— SERVES 6 ————

PROFITEROLES WITH CHOCOLATE SAUCE

*A great French classic: light choux pastry cases filled with
vanilla ice cream and coated with hot chocolate sauce.*

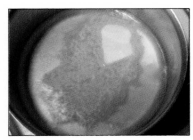

Step 1

Step 2

Step 3

Step 3

□

OPPOSITE

PROFITEROLES
WITH CHOCOLATE
SAUCE

CHOUX PASTRY

□ 300ml/½ pint water   □ 75g/3oz butter   □ Pinch salt
□ 150g/6oz plain flour, sifted   □ 5 large eggs, beaten

CHOCOLATE SAUCE

□ 150g/6oz dark chocolate, melted
□ 100ml/4fl. oz whipping cream   □ 30g/2 tbsps sugar

FILLING

□ 600ml/1 pint vanilla ice cream

1. In a saucepan, bring the water to the boil, add the butter and the pinch of salt.

2. Remove from the heat as soon as the butter has melted and beat in the flour, a little at a time. Allow to dry out a little.

3. Beat in the beaten egg little by little, retaining a little for brushing, and fill a piping bag fitted with a plain tip with the mixture.

4. Heat the oven to 220°C/425°F/Gas Mark 7. Grease 2 baking sheets, and pipe out 12 small balls of choux pastry, spreading the balls well apart. Mix the remaining beaten egg with a little water and brush over the choux pastry balls.

5. Cook these for 10 minutes and then reduce the heat to 180°C/350°F/Gas Mark 4 and cook for approximately 20 minutes more – the balls should double in size and be golden brown.

6. Remove from the oven and pierce them to let the steam escape. Turn off the oven, leave the door open, and put the profiteroles back in the open oven to dry out for approximately 10 minutes.

7. Melt the chocolate and the sugar together over a pan of boiling water, then stir in the cream.

8. Slice open the pastry cases, fill with ice cream and pour over the chocolate sauce.

TIME   Preparation takes about 25 minutes and cooking takes 1 hour.

COOK'S TIP   Cut out the base of each choux ball, fill with ice cream and then turn upside down to serve, with the sauce poured over.

WATCHPOINT   Melt the chocolate, cream and sugar over a very gentle heat, stirring continuously, and remove from the heat as soon as the mixture is completely smooth.

—— SERVES 6 ——

BANANAS IN ORANGE SAUCE

The delicious caramel orange sauce makes this a perfect dish hot or cold.

Step 1

Step 1

Step 2

☐ 6 large bananas, peeled ☐ 45ml/3 tbsps sugar
☐ 30g/2 tbsps butter ☐ 15ml/1 tbsp cream sherry
☐ 30ml/2 tbsps orange liqueur ☐ Juice of 2 oranges

1. In a heavy-based saucepan, melt together and then boil the butter and the sugar until a white caramel forms.

2. Stir in the sherry, liqueur and orange juice, and allow the mixture to reduce a little.

3. Cut the bananas into even rounds and add them to the sauce.

4. With a tablespoon, remove the sauce-coated bananas and arrange them on small individual plates. Make rose shapes by interlacing the bananas, then pour over the remaining sauce.

TIME   Preparation takes about 10 minutes and cooking takes 10 minutes.

SERVING IDEA   Presenting the bananas in a rose pattern is, of course, optional, but so much nicer to the eye.

COOK'S TIP   Finely shred about 6 fresh mint leaves and add these just before serving; they give a lovely flavour.

VARIATION   To obtain a really authentic flavour, use French Rivesalts in place of the sherry.

☐

OPPOSITE

BANANAS IN ORANGE SAUCE

——— SERVES 6 ———

LEMON TART

*Both tangy yet smooth, the lemon filling in this
tart is mouthwateringly delicious.*

Step 3

Step 3

SWEET DOUGH

☐ 225g/8 oz plain flour, sifted

☐ 100g/4oz butter, cut into cubes   ☐ 100g/4oz sugar

☐ 1 egg, beaten   ☐ Pinch salt

LEMON FILLING

☐ 100g/4oz butter   ☐ 150g/6oz sugar

☐ 5 eggs, beaten   ☐ Juice of 2 lemons   ☐ Zest of ½ lemon

1. Place the flour in a mixing bowl, add the salt and rub in the butter with your fingers. Stir in the sugar. Mix in the egg and form the dough into a ball. Place in the refrigerator for 5 to 10 minutes.

2. Roll out the dough on a floured surface, line a pie pan with the pastry, and bake unfilled in a moderately hot oven until cooked – approximately 20 minutes.

3. Mix all the ingredients for the lemon filling together in a saucepan. Put over a gentle heat and stir continuously for 10 minutes. The mixture will become quite thick.

4. Allow to cool and chill slightly in the refrigerator. Stir well and then fill the pastry shell. Keep the tart covered in the refrigerator until required.

TIME   Preparation takes about 20 minutes, cooking takes approximately 30 minutes and chilling about 30 minutes.

VARIATION   Use small individual flan cases. The pastry will cook much more quickly – approximately 10 minutes.

SERVING IDEA   Peel a lemon and cut the flesh into thin slices. Remove the pips and place on the finished tart.

☐

OPPOSITE

LEMON TART

SERVES 6

PEACH MELBA

The real peach melba, with fresh raspberry sauce.

Step 1

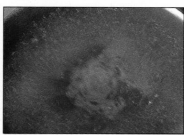

Step 1

Step 2

□ 6 fresh peaches or canned peaches in syrup
□ 600ml/1 pint vanilla ice cream   □ 450g/1 lb fresh raspberries
□ 150g/6oz sugar   □ 15ml/1 tbsp kirsch   □ Juice of ½ lemon

1. In a saucepan, bring to the boil 300ml/½ pint water, the sugar, lemon juice, kirsch and the raspberries. Boil briskly for 5 minutes, then set aside to cool.

2. Once cool, blend smooth in a blender, then pass through a fine sieve. Chill in the refrigerator.

3. Place each peach in a small coupe, add a ball of ice cream and pour over a little sauce.

TIME   Preparation takes about 20 minutes and cooking takes approximately 8 minutes. Chill for at least 15 minutes.

VARIATION   Use frozen raspberries if fresh are not in season, and replace the kirsch with different fruit liqueurs.

□

OPPOSITE

PEACH MELBA

FRESH FRUIT IN
RED WINE SYRUP

A lovely summery dessert using as many different
fruits as possible, and coated in a red wine sauce.

☐ 1 litre red wine (Beaujolais or similar)   ☐ 450g/1lb sugar
☐ 200ml/6fl. oz water   ☐ 1 whole clove
☐ 1 stick cinnamon   ☐ Zest of 1 orange
☐ A selection of fresh fruit, peeled, pitted, sliced
or halved as necessary

1. Make the syrup by boiling together the wine, water, sugar, whole clove, zest and cinnamon for at least 30 minutes.

2. Remove from the heat and set aside to cool. Chill in the refrigerator.

3. Prepare the fruit and present on a serving dish.

4. Remove the cinnamon and the whole clove. Pour the chilled syrup over the fruit and serve.

Step 3

Step 3

TIME   Preparation will take approximately 10 minutes, depending on the fruit you have chosen, and cooking will take at least 30 minutes. Chill for 1 hour.

VARIATION   Once the syrup has chilled, add the fruit and marinate for 1 day in the refrigerator.

WATCHPOINT   Use only very fresh fruit.

SERVING IDEA   Garnish the salad with fresh mint leaves.

☐

OPPOSITE

FRESH FRUIT IN
RED WINE SYRUP

———— SERVES 4 ————

GATEAU GIENNOIS

*A nutty-flavoured, fluffy-topped
tart, with a surprise raspberry centre.*

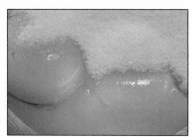

Step 2

Step 4

Step 5

☐ 225g/8oz shortcrust pastry ☐ 3 egg yolks
☐ 100g/4oz sugar ☐ 65g/2½ oz shelled walnuts, ground
☐ 2 egg whites, stiffly beaten ☐ 60ml/4 tbsps raspberry jam

1. Roll out the pastry on a lightly floured surface. Line 4 individual pie pans with the pastry, pricking the base and sides with a fork.

2. Beat together the egg yolks and the sugar until white.

3. Stir in the ground walnuts.

4. Gently incorporate the beaten egg whites using a metal spoon.

5. Place 15ml/1 tbsp of jam in the base of each tart and spoon over the mixture evenly between the 4 tarts.

6. Cook in a moderate oven 180°C/350°F/Gas Mark 4 until the pastry is cooked and the filling lightly puffed. Serve as soon as possible.

TIME   Preparation takes about 25 minutes and cooking time is approximately 25 to 35 minutes.

VARIATION   Use ground almonds or hazelnuts instead of walnuts.

☐

OPPOSITE

GATEAU GIENNOIS

TARTES FINES AUX POIRES

Tempting tarts consisting of a fine layer of flaky pastry covered in sliced pears, served with a sweet sauce.

Step 2

☐ 450g/1lb flaky pastry ☐ 4 large pears, peeled, cored and sliced ☐ ½ bottle sweet white wine (Montbazillac if possible) ☐ 100g/4oz butter, diced ☐ 30g/2 tbsps sugar

1. Begin by rolling our the pastry and cutting it into 6 even rounds. Place these rounds on 2 lightly-greased cookie sheets.

2. Place the pear slices evenly and decoratively over the pastry. Sprinkle over the sugar.

3. Cook in a moderately hot oven, 180°C/350°F/Gas Mark 4, until cooked, brown and crispy – approximately 20 to 25 minutes.

4. In a large, heavy-based saucepan, over a high heat, allow the wine to boil, reduce and thicken.

5. When the wine is syrupy, remove from the heat and stir in the diced butter.

6. Serve the sauce either poured over the tarts or separately in a small sauce boat.

TIME   Preparation takes about 10 minutes and cooking takes 35 minutes.

SERVING IDEA   Serve with a ball of pear sorbet, and garnish with fresh mint.

COOK'S TIP   Serve the sauce as soon as you have added the butter, and don't let the sauce get cold.

☐

OPPOSITE

TARTES FINES
AUX POIRES

SERVES 4

POMMES SAUTEES AU MUSCAT

Sautéed apples with currants.

Step 1

Step 2

Step 2

☐ 4 Golden Delicious apples, peeled and quartered
☐ 50g/2oz butter ☐ 45ml/3 tbsps currants
☐ 100ml/4fl. oz Muscat ☐ 50g/2oz sugar
☐ 5ml/1 tsp cinnamon

1. Melt the butter in a large frying pan, sauté the apples, add the sugar and allow to caramelise slightly.

2. Sprinkle over the currants and cook for a few seconds more.

2. Deglaze the pan with the Muscat, sprinkle over the cinnamon and serve immediately.

TIME Preparation takes about 5 minutes and cooking takes approximately 10 minutes.

COOK'S TIP Soak the currants in a cup of tea (without milk), draining before using.

WATCHPOINT The frying pan should not be returned to the heat once it has been deglazed.

SERVING IDEA Serve with a glass of chilled Muscat.

VARIATION Substitute the Muscat with a sweet white wine.

☐

OPPOSITE

POMMES SAUTEES
AU MUSCAT